Weather Wise

Thunder and Lightning

Helen Cox Cannons

Raintree

Raintree is an imprint of Capstone Global Library Limited, a company incorporated in England and Wales having its registered office at 7 Pilgrim Street, London, EC4V 6LB – Registered company number: 6695582

www.raintreepublishers.co.uk
myorders@raintreepublishers.co.uk

Text © Capstone Global Library Limited 2015
First published in hardback in 2014
The moral rights of the proprietor have been asserted.

Edited by Siân Smith and John-Paul Wilkins
Designed by Philippa Jenkins
Picture research by Ruth Blair
Production by Victoria Fitzgerald
Originated by Capstone Global Library Ltd
Printed and bound in China

ISBN 978 1 4062 8481 2
18 17 16 15 14
10 9 8 7 6 5 4 3 2 1

British Library Cataloguing in Publication Data
A full catalogue record for this book is available from the British Library.

Acknowledgements
We would like to thank the following for permission to reproduce photographs: Corbis: JGI/Jamie Grill/Blend Images, 19, Olix Wirtinger, 20; Dreamstime: Bandesz, 18, 23 (bottom), Jhaz, 5; iStockphoto: cschoeps, 15; NASA: 22 (left); Shutterstock: Andrey Prokhorov, 16, Balazs Kovacs, 12, 23 (middle), David W. Leindecker, 14, Igor Zh., 22 (right), Mihai Simonia, 7, muratart, 13, Pictureguy, 4, Piotr Krzeslak, 21, Scott Prokop, 17, szpeti, 6, 23 (top), violetkaipa, cover

We would like to thank John Horel for his invaluable help in the preparation of this book.

Every effort has been made to contact copyright holders of material reproduced in this book. Any omissions will be rectified in subsequent printings if notice is given to the publisher.

Contents

What is thunder?

Thunder is the sound of **lightning**. You cannot see thunder, but you can hear it.

Thunder can sound like a low rumble or a loud crack.

What is lightning?

Lightning is a bright flash of **electricity** in the sky.

Lightning comes from a cloud.
A storm with thunder or lightning
is called a thunderstorm.

How does lightning happen?

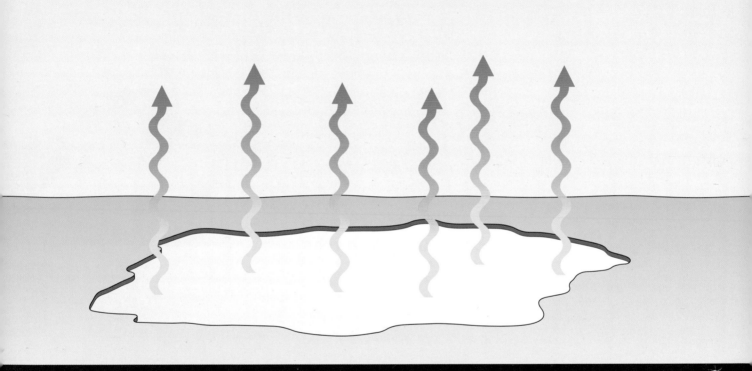

When the Sun warms water, some water becomes a gas called **vapour**. Vapour rises into the air.

The rising vapour cools and forms a cloud. As more vapour rises, the cloud gets bigger and bigger.

Frozen raindrops inside the cloud start to bump into each other.

As they bump into each other, the frozen raindrops make electricity. This electricity turns into lightning.

When does lightning happen?

Lightning can happen when it is warm.

Lightning can happen when it rains.

Types of lightning

Sometimes lightning stays in a cloud.

Sometimes lightning strikes the ground.

Keeping safe

Lightning can be very dangerous.

Lightning often strikes high places or tall things.

If you hear thunder, it means that lightning is close by.

It is best to stay inside when you hear thunder.

What is good about thunder and lightning?

Thunder and lightning can be exciting.

Thunderstorms help us see the power of weather.

Did you know?

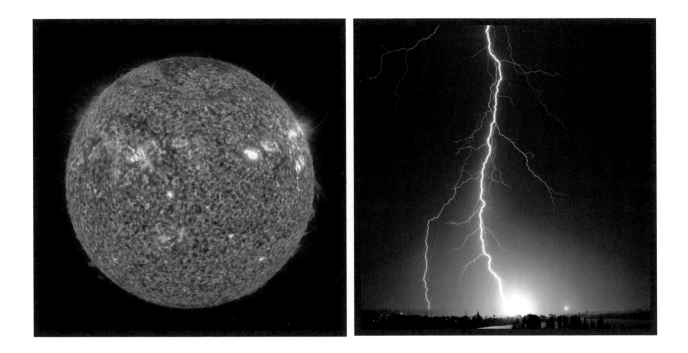

Lightning is about six times hotter than the Sun!

Picture glossary

electricity form of energy

lightning bright flash
of electricity in the sky

thunder the sound
of lightning

vapour gas created
by heating water

Index

Notes for parents and teachers

Before reading
Assess background knowledge. Ask: What are thunder and lightning? Where do thunder and lightning come from?

After reading
Recall and reflection: Ask children if their ideas about thunder and lightning at the beginning were correct. What else do they wonder about?

Sentence knowledge: Ask children to find sentences that end with three different punctuation marks. How does punctuation change the way they read sentences?

Word recognition: Ask children to point at the word *strikes* on page 15. Can they also find it on page 17?